bus

We are cruising through the town!

taxicab scooter

THE ORIGINAL INDESTRUCTIBLES®

For ages 0 and up!

Books babies can really sink their gums into!

Baby's driving down the road. Look, a truck!

Baby's flying in the air. Wow, there's a plane!

Baby's sailing on the sea—along with a ship, a sailboat, and a submarine!

Learn all about things that go in a book that's INDESTRUCTIBLE.

DEAR PARENTS: INDESTRUCTIBLES are built for the way babies "read": with their hands and mouths. INDESTRUCTIBLES won't rip or tear and are 100% washable. They're made for baby to hold, grab, chew, pull, and bend.

CHEW ALL THESE AND MORE!

Copyright © 2017 by Indestructibles, LLC. Used under license. Illustrations copyright © 2017 by Workman Publishing. All rights reserved. Library of Congress Cataloging-in-Publication Data is available. Workman Kids is an imprint of Workman Publishing, a division of Hachette Book Group, Inc.

The Workman name and logo are registered trademarks of Hachette Book Group, Inc.

Distributed in the United Kingdom by Hachette Book Group, UK, Carmelite House, 50 Victoria Embankment, London EC4Y 0DZ.

Distributed in Europe by Hachette Livre, 58 rue Jean Bleuzen, 92 178 Vanves Cedex, France.

Contact special.markets@hbgusa.com regarding special discounts for bulk purchases.

All INDESTRUCTIBLES books have been safety-tested and meet or exceed ASTM-F963 and CPSIA guidelines.

INDESTRUCTIBLES is a registered trademark of Indestructibles, LLC.

Cover © 2024 Hachette Book Group, Inc.
First Edition March 2017 I 20 19 18 17
Printed in Shenzhen, China I IMFP

$5.99 US / $7.99 Can.
ISBN 978-0-7611-9362-3

WORKMAN PUBLISHING • Hachette Book Group, Inc., 1290 Avenue of the Americas, New York, NY 10104 • indestructiblesinc.com